STOP!

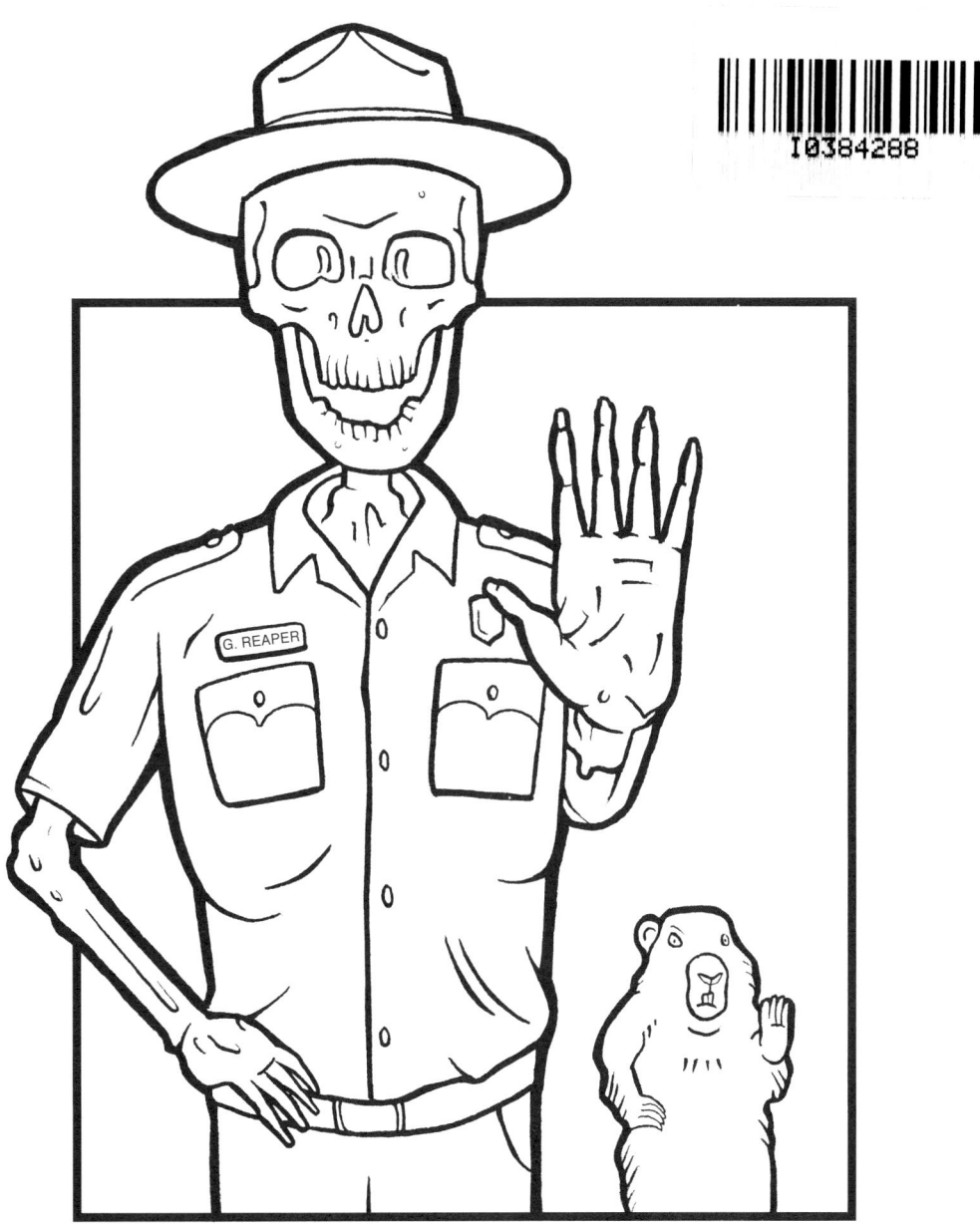

This coloring book isn't for everyone! It depicts scenes of graphic violence, including disembowelment, dismemberment, electrocution, and immolation. You've been warned!

ISBN: 978-0-692-74725-4

Published by ☠ Caput Mortuum Books, Ranchester, Wyoming

©2016 by Andy Robbins
http://www.andyrobbinsart.com

All rights reserved. This book may not be reproduced in whole or in part by any means (with the exception of short quotes for the purpose of review) without the permission of the publisher.

You may order extra copies of this book by calling Farcountry Press toll free at (800) 821-3874.

Produced by Sweetgrass Books
PO Box 5630, Helena, MT 59604; (800) 821-3874
www.sweetgrassbooks.com

The views expressed by the author/publisher in this book do not necessarily represent the views of, nor should be attributed to, Sweetgrass Books. Sweetgrass Books is not responsible for the content of the author/publisher's work.

 Produced and printed in the United States of America.

YELLOWSTONE NATIONAL PARK

A Cautionary Coloring Book

BEAUTIFUL, ISN'T IT? Most visitors to the Park will happily enjoy its abundant wildlife, scenic views, and fantastic recreational activities with no injury to themselves. Others won't be so lucky. Use this coloring book to learn about the Park's natural features and amazing animals... and how to avoid dying during your vacation!

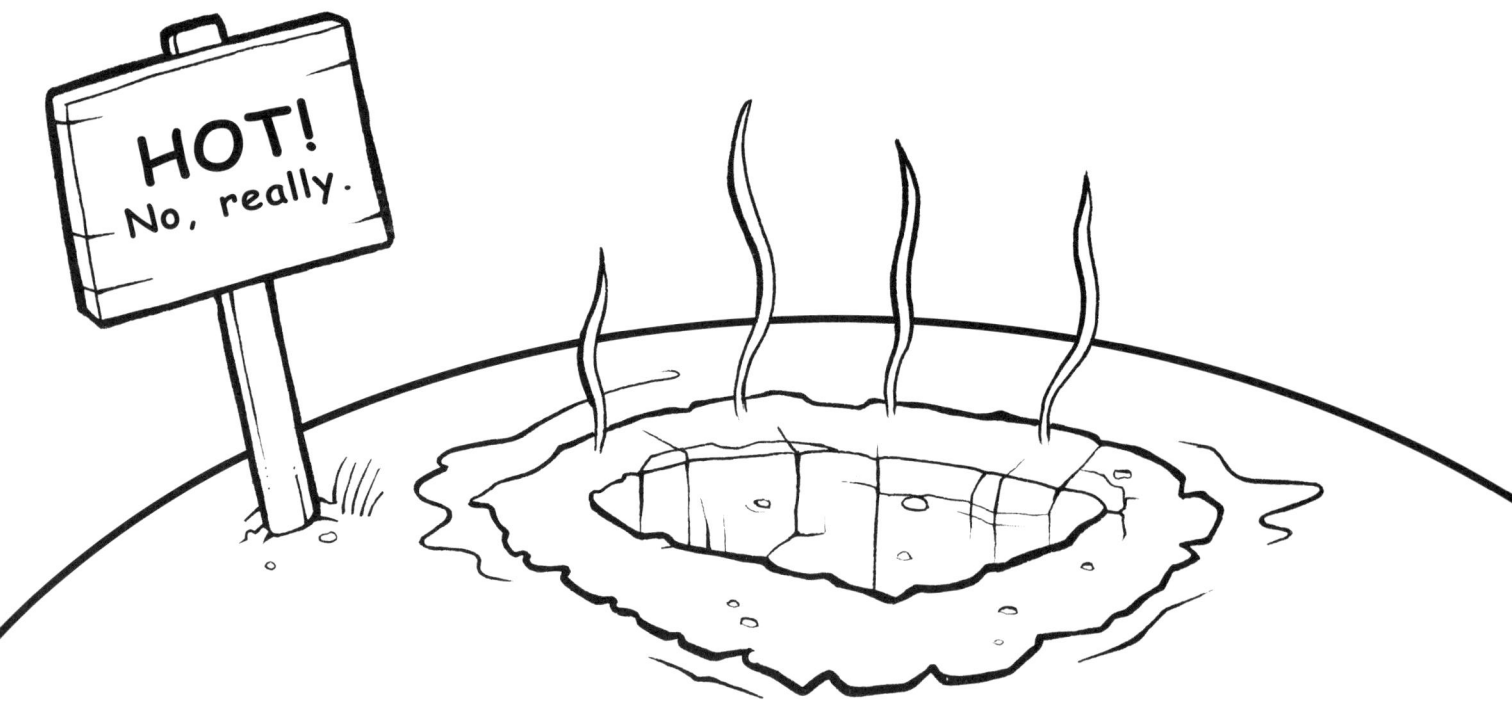

HOT STUFF! The hot springs of Yellowstone can reach temperatures in excess of 250 degrees Fahrenheit. While those pristine pools might look like oversized hot tubs, they are far, far hotter than the human body can withstand. Even one of the cooler pools can boil your skin clean off after just a few seconds of submersion, so even quickly rescued victims usually die. Sadly, this gruesome (and well-posted!) fact hasn't stopped Park visitors from accidently falling, and even intentionally diving, into the thermal features over the years. The deaths of dog owners who have jumped into hot springs to rescue their pets are at least partially to blame for Yellowstone's current policy of no dogs in the Park.

ANIMAL SPOTLIGHT: Bald Eagle (Haliaeetus leucocephalus). As both the national bird and the national animal of the United States, the bald eagle has a lot resting on his shoulders. You might see this large predatory bird flying over Yellowstone Lake during the summer months or buzzing the Park's rivers for fish to eat.

ANIMAL SPOTLIGHT: American Pika (Ochotona princeps). The Pika resides almost everywhere in Yellowstone, though the Park Service recommends keeping your eyes peeled for these critters in the Tower and Mammoth areas. You might also hear their high-pitched alarm calls; they sound like squeaky toys! About the size of a guinea pig, the pika makes his home in rocky areas, where he actively seeks plants to eat throughout the year. Though pikas look like rodents, they are not. They instead share their scientific order with rabbits and hares.

CAN PIKA KILL YOU? No. But their cuteness might!

SUGGESTED COLORS: Scalded Pink, Boiled Purple, Bacteria Bloom Yellow

HURK! While it should come as no surprise that Yellowstone is home to several toxic mushrooms, the water hemlock plant, regarded as the most poisonous plant in North America, can also be found within its borders. Though carrot-like in appearance, consuming the water hemlock has decidedly uncarrot-like results: death from respiratory failure can occur in as few as fifteen minutes. Besides a swift death, other symptoms of water hemlock poisoning include seizures, vomiting, and abdominal pain. Several Park visitors have died in this fashion after consuming the plant. Seriously, if you don't know what it is, don't put it in your mouth!

Animal Spotlight: Mule Deer (Odocoileus hemionus). Found throughout Yellowstone, mule deer number nearly 2000 in the summer months. You might find them snacking on their favorite grasses and shrubs while craftily avoiding the water hemlock.

Can a mule deer kill you? Doubtful. Though a buck can weigh several hundred pounds and sport impressive antlers, deer only rarely harm people. Still, mule deer can exhibit aggressive behavior during the fall breeding and spring fawning seasons. Give 'em a little distance and let them do their thing!

Suggested Colors: Bilious Green, Suffocatin' Blue, Ghastly White

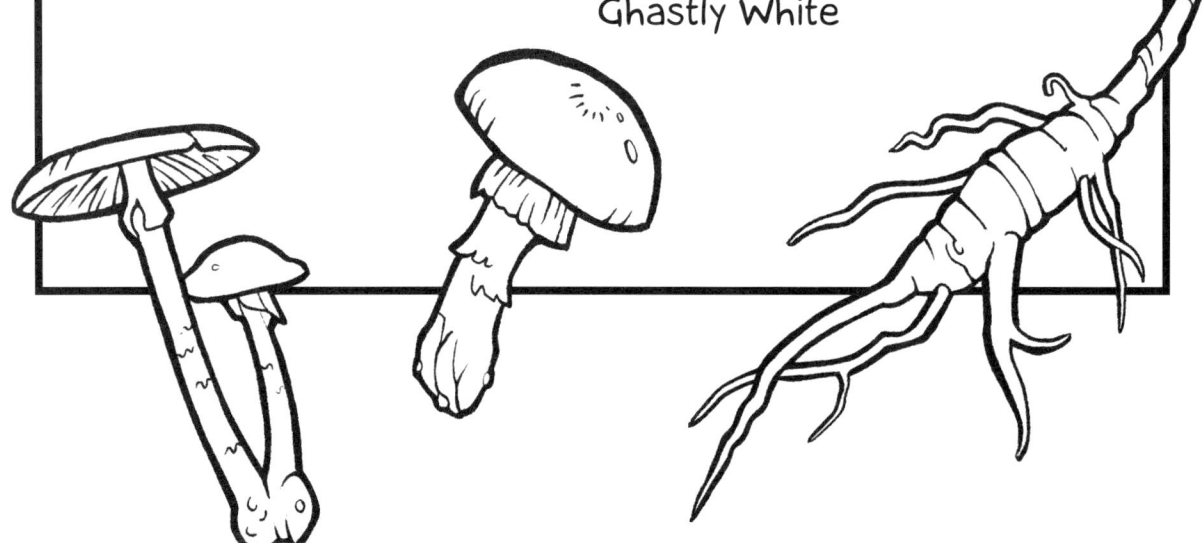

RAMMING SPEED! What does it feel like to be impaled by a 2000 pound horned freight train? Ask the ever-increasing number of visitors who have gotten too close to Yellowstone's famous bison. While the bison you see from your car window might look harmless enough, rest assured: bison can move fast when annoyed and are capable of goring, disemboweling, and killing tourists who have crowded in for a closer look (or heaven forbid, for a selfie with the animal—something that resulted in a 2015 attack). It's important to remember that none of Yellowstone's animals are tame, and there are no fences or barriers to keep you safe. Photograph the bison from a respectable distance, and be mindful should one start to move in your direction!

ANIMAL SPOTLIGHT: American Bison (Bison bison). Tens of millions of bison once roamed the plains of the United States, but were systematically slaughtered by overzealous hunters. Today, nearly 150,000 of their descendants survive, both in protected places like Yellowstone and in commercial settings where bison are raised for their meat, much like cattle. In fact, you can now order a bison or beefalo (a bison/domestic cattle cross) burger in many restaurants—tasty! The term "buffalo" is often used interchangeably with bison, but is a bit of a misnomer. The American bison is only distantly related to "true" buffalo like the water buffalo.

CAN A BISON KILL YOU? Heck yes. Though not generally malevolent, bison are huge, horned, and hard-hitting.

SUGGESTED COLORS: Selfie Stick Silver, Kidney Pink, Bowel Burgundy

CRASH TEST DUMMIES! Four million people a year visit Yellowstone. Many of them arrive in their own cars, trucks, and recreational vehicles. Combine that with winding two lane roads and animals begging to be photographed alongside the asphalt and you've got a recipe for disaster. Twenty deaths in Yellowstone between 1998 to 2006 were attributed to motor vehicle collisions, though the tally could be substantially higher as that number does not include visitors transported out of the Park who later died from their injuries. While it might be more titillating to imagine dying in the claws of a grizzly bear, a Yellowstone visitor is far more likely to die behind the wheel of the family car. Drive safely!

ANIMAL SPOTLIGHT: Elk (Cervus canadensis). Yellowstone and its surrounding ecosystem provide habitat for a large number of elk—up to 20,000 by some estimates! Good thing, too, because many of the Park's predators enjoy eating them. The Park Service suggests you look for elk in the Lamar Valley, Elk Park, and the Mammoth area.

CAN AN ELK KILL YOU? Most likely. Weighing in at 700 pounds and armed with antlers and hooves, a bull elk could stomp you into a bloody puddle. To date, such a fatality hasn't happened in Yellowstone. Attacks, however, are commonplace.

SUGGESTED COLORS: Ejected Orange, High Speed Cobalt, Chrome

BLUB BLUB! Maybe it's our ancient aquatic roots: humans love playing in the water. Drowning in it, not so much, but they do that in prodigious numbers, too. With attractions like Yellowstone Lake and the Firehole River, Yellowstone offers visitors many opportunities to indulge their inner Neptune. Unfortunately, not all of those who brave the Park's waters come home alive. Many of Yellowstone's drowning deaths occur in its lakes, where unwary boaters capsize during abrupt summer storms. Others drown while fishing Yellowstone's rivers and streams. If you go out on the water, make sure to wear a life jacket—it just might save your life!

ANIMAL SPOTLIGHT: Artic Grayling (Thymallus arcticus), Yellowstone and Westslope Cutthroat Troat (Oncorhynchus clarkii), and Mountain Whitefish (Prosopium williamsoni). Most of the fish you'll find in Yellowstone's waters were introduced over the years, changing the ecology of the lakes and rivers. Though you will find other types of trout in the Park, these three sport fish are true natives.

CAN ONE OF THESE FISH KILL YOU? No. Fish have no people-killing skills.

SUGGESTED COLORS: Bloated Blue, Rotten Red, Sea Green

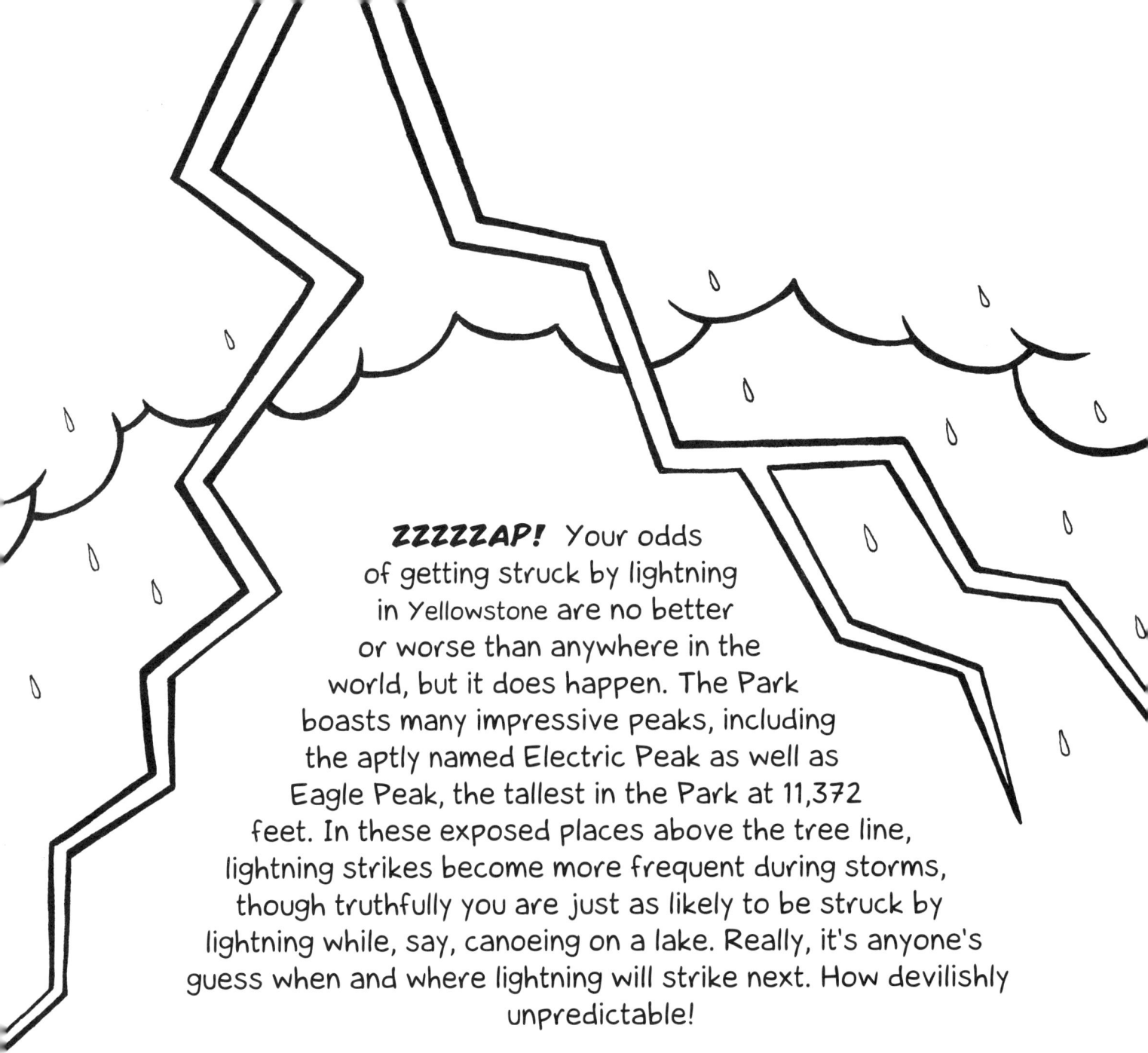

ZZZZZAP! Your odds of getting struck by lightning in Yellowstone are no better or worse than anywhere in the world, but it does happen. The Park boasts many impressive peaks, including the aptly named Electric Peak as well as Eagle Peak, the tallest in the Park at 11,372 feet. In these exposed places above the tree line, lightning strikes become more frequent during storms, though truthfully you are just as likely to be struck by lightning while, say, canoeing on a lake. Really, it's anyone's guess when and where lightning will strike next. How devilishly unpredictable!

ANIMAL SPOTLIGHT: Yellow-bellied Marmot (Marmota flaviventris). The Yellow-bellied Marmot isn't a coward—he's named that because of the yellow fur on his belly! He does tend to get fat and then sleep a lot though, sometimes for up to eight months of the year. Known as "whistle pigs" for their loud vocalization, these large rodents dwell near rocks, where they can construct burrows less visible to predators. The marmot eats whatever he can get his paws on so don't leave any junk food behind for him to find!

CAN A MARMOT KILL YOU? You're more likely to be killed by lightning than injured by a marmot.

SUGGESTED COLORS: Electric Blue, Stormy Black, Marmot Belly Yella

ALL YOU CAN EAT! The Grizzly Bear (Ursus arctos horribilis) is a meat-shredding machine, capable of completely disassembling its prey, including the occasional human, before devouring it. Weighing up to 700 pounds, a male grizzly has 4 inch claws and can sprint as fast as 45 miles per hour. Over the years, bears have killed nine visitors to Yellowstone and injured dozens more. You can minimize the likelihood of bear attacks by carrying pepper spray, following proper camping protocols, and avoiding areas that bears are known to frequent. Still, the Park stresses that "your safety cannot be guaranteed" when it comes to bears. This apex predator can and will kill a human with ease. If you're lucky, you'll already be dead when the bear starts to eat you!

NOTE: Both grizzly bears and black bears inhabit Yellowstone. Though not as prone to murderous rampages as its cousin, the black bear should also be treated with respect.

ANIMAL SPOTLIGHT: Least Chipmunk (Tamias minimus) and Golden-Mantled Ground Squirrel (Callospermophilus lateralis). The chipmunk and the ground squirrel are two of the more common rodents you might spy during your visit to Yellowstone. Both have cheek pouches for storing food, and both hibernate during the Park's colder months. Please don't feed them any human food, no matter how adamantly they ask.

CAN A CHIPMUNK OR SQUIRREL KILL YOU? Nope... and nope.

SUGGESTED COLORS: Runny Red, Meaty Pink, Beary Brown

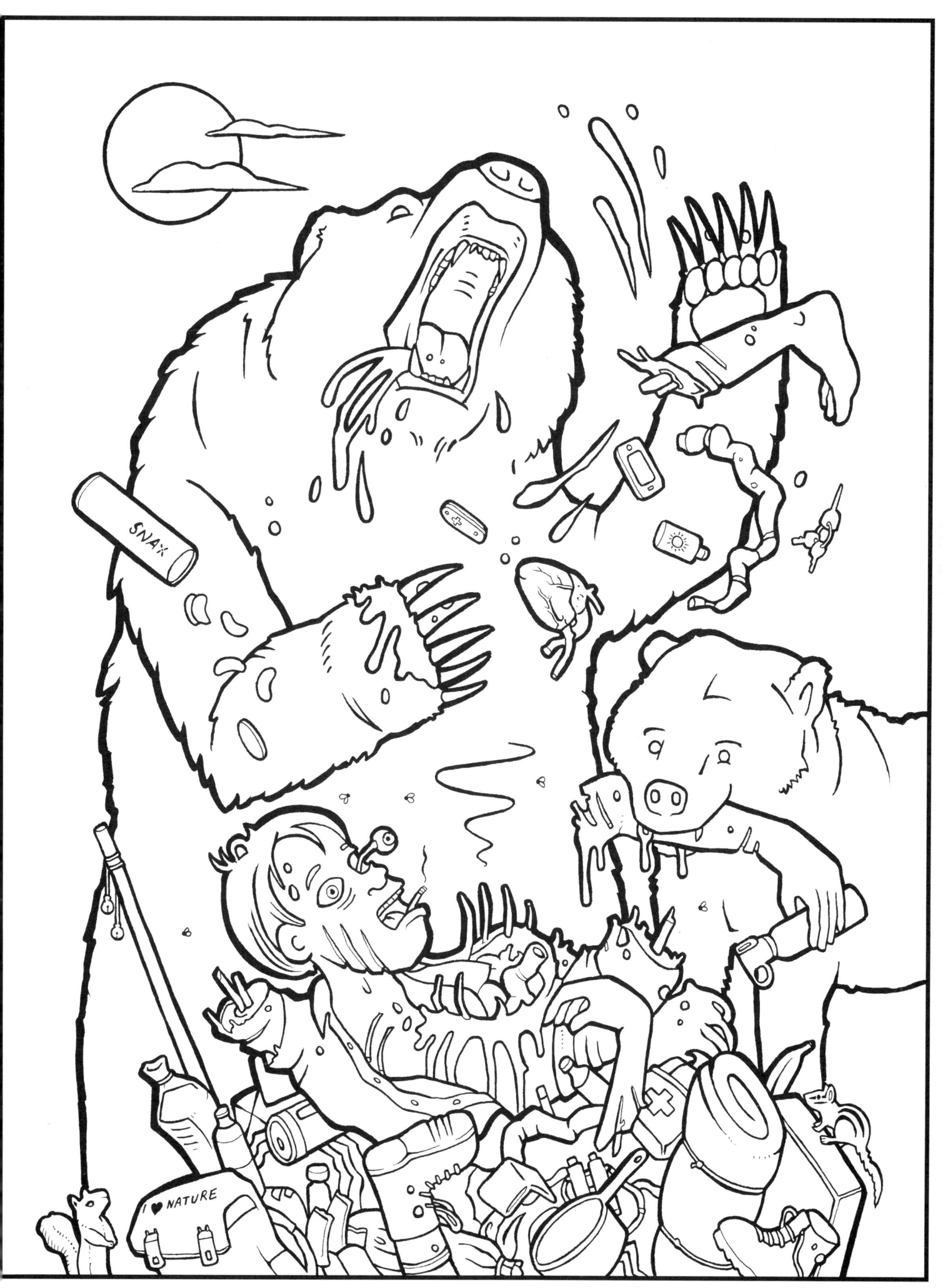

BRRRRRRR! It gets cold in Yellowstone. Real cold. The record low is -66 degrees Fahrenheit and overnight winter temperatures commonly fall well below zero. Even when its not below freezing, some areas in the Park remain chilly throughout the year. While no one has frozen to death in Yellowstone lately, the influx of modern winter visitors increases the likelihood that someone will die in this way again soon. Protect yourself by preparing for the elements and knowing your route before setting out.

Animal Spotlight: Gray Wolf (Canis lupus). Though once nearly hunted to extinction throughout the Rockies, the gray wolf has seen a resurgence in Yellowstone thanks to controversial re-introduction efforts beginning in 1995. Yellowstone is now home to around 500 wolves, most visible at dawn and dusk in the Lamar Valley. The wolves are known to hunt the Park's elk in packs; they also prey on deer, small mammals, and occasionally, unlucky livestock. A male wolf can weigh as much as 130 pounds and requires 7 pounds of food per day to thrive.

Can a Wolf Kill You? Sure can! You wouldn't want to find yourself alone in the woods with a hungry wolf pack at your heels. That said, there have been no wolf-related fatalities in Yellowstone, and even reports of wolf attacks are questionable.

Suggested Colors: Frostbite Violet, Icy Blue, Whiteout White

TRAMPLED! The moose (Alces alces) may look too goofy to do you harm, but there's a reason why Park Rangers will tell you that moose are more dangerous than grizzly bears. While moose prefer to leave you alone, they can become brazen—and grouchy—when hungry. Mother moose, known as cows, are especially testy when it comes to the well-being of their calves and will go to great lengths to protect their offspring. That includes trampling you until you're no longer a perceived threat. So, while the moose may look silly, remember that she is large and in charge.

ANIMAL SPOTLIGHT: Prairie Rattlesnake (Crotalus viridis). Yellowstone only has one deadly venomous snake in its borders, but it's a doozy. The Prairie Rattlesnake lives in low, dry areas of the Park, feeding on small mammals and birds. Snake bites in the Park are extremely rare, but listen for the rattlesnake's rattle all the same!

CAN A RATTLESNAKE KILL YOU? You bet! The venom of a rattlesnake can cause serious tissue damage—even death—if left untreated. Quickly administered antivenoms usually reverse the effects of a bite, however, and death by snake is an uncommon way to check out.

SUGGESTED COLORS: Pummeled Puce, Squished Scarlet, Moose Maroon

WATCH OUT FOR THAT FIRST STEP!

From Yellowstone's many overlooks one can contemplate nature in all its stunning splendor. But don't get so enamored with the scenery that you lose your footing! Whether leaning over a handrail in a busy tourist area or free climbing to a backcountry ledge for a better view, death by falling has claimed the lives of many in Yellowstone, and this trend is likely to continue. So, the next time you think about jumping the railing for that perfect picture of the Grand Canyon of the Yellowstone, remember: it's a long way down!

ANIMAL SPOTLIGHT: Rocky Mountain Bighorn Sheep (Ovis Canadensis). Yellowstone has a population of roughly 200 bighorn sheep, which can be seen along the cliffs of the Yellowstone River and in the northern canyons of the Park. Males, known as rams, grow large curling horns, which they use to establish mating dominance through head-battering contests. Females also grow horns, though smaller in size. If you're wondering whether or not bighorn sheep ever fall off those cliffs themselves, yes, it happens. Even these agile animals fall prey to gravity now and then.

CAN A BIGHORN SHEEP KILL YOU? Probably not. However, rams have been known to clobber humans (and their vehicles) during the November mating season, so it would be prudent not to turn your back on a sheep if you happen to be standing on the edge of cliff!

SUGGESTED COLORS: Brainy Beige, Compound Fracture Red, Sandstone

THAR SHE BLOWS! If you're visiting Yellowstone, you're standing on or near the caldera of a massive supervolcano! All of those erupting geysers and steaming pools are a reminder of how much molten rock lies just below the surface, waiting for a seismic shift to explode and reduce you and everything nearby to ash. If such an eruption were to occur, you'd need to be several states away to survive. We're talking potential extinction-level-event stuff here. The good news is that such an event—as far as scientists can predict—is unlikely to occur during your visit to Yellowstone. Of course, one never knows for sure!

ANIMAL SPOTLIGHT: Coyote (Canis latrans). The wily coyote makes his living anyway he can. This adaptable animal thrives in Yellowstone, though its population has declined as wolf populations rise. Coyotes often travel in pairs or packs as they hunt small mammals. But really, they're not too picky. So, while you're unlikely to see a coyote near your campfire, you can be sure that he isn't far away, watching from the shadows for an opportunity to steal your dinner.

CAN A COYOTE KILL YOU? Yes! As civilization encroaches into wilderness areas, attacks by coyotes have become more frequent. Though such attacks are not often fatal, coyotes have killed humans in recent years. No such encounters have been reported in Yellowstone, however, maybe because the Park's coyotes have plenty of room to roam.

SUGGESTED COLORS: Cataclysmic Crimson, Molten Orange, Vaporized Vermilion

IN THE END... Yellowstone National Park offers many ways for the careless or unlucky visitor to meet his untimely end. From mundane accidents to freakishly horrific events, the Park really can be a deathtrap. Sure, some of Yellowstone's misfortunes are entirely preventable; others not so much. But you can reduce your chances of dying in Yellowstone by giving wildlife a wide berth, respecting age-old killers like water and gravity, and understanding that the Park's rules apply to everyone (yes, even you!).

Realistically, you're not going to do any dying during your trip to Yellowstone. You'll probably be too busy enjoying one of the most awesome natural places in the world to even think about death. But should you to perish in the Park, know that you aren't the first, and you certainly won't be the last to do so!

Be safe and enjoy your visit to Yellowstone National Park!

SUGGESTED COLORS: Sunset Orange, Glorious Green, Nonviolent Violet

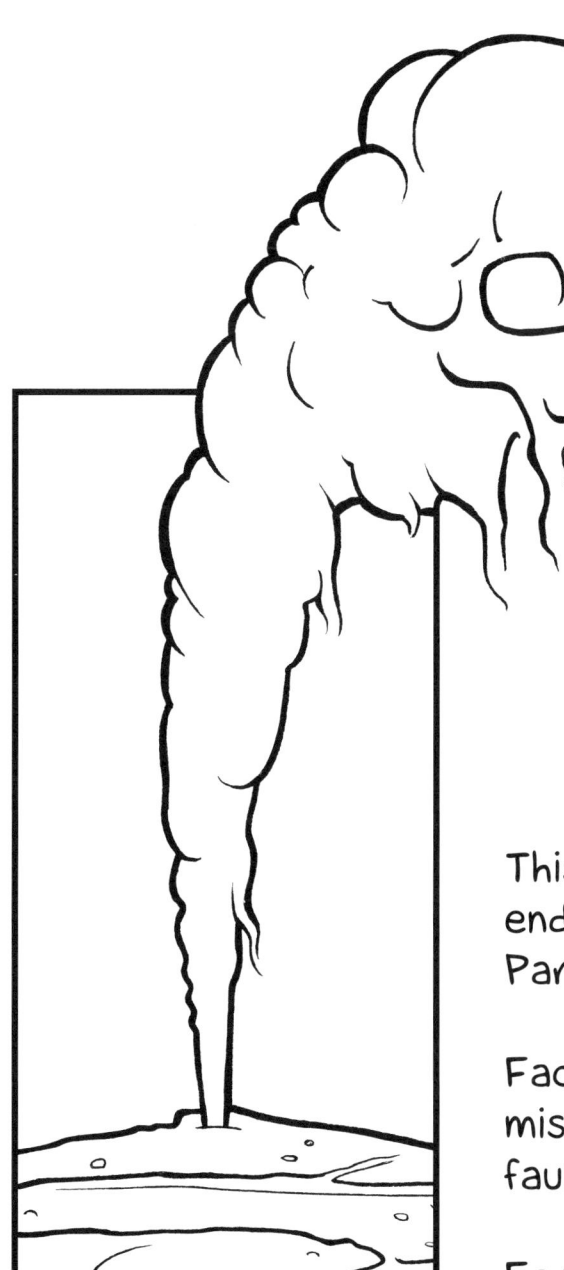

This book is not associated with or endorsed by Yellowstone National Park or the National Park Service.

Factual mistakes or misrepresentations are solely the fault of the author.

For the definitive book about dying in Yellowstone National Park, check out <u>Death in Yellowstone: Accidents and Foolhardiness in the First National Park</u> by Lee H. Whittlesey.